WRATH
A DICTIONARY FOR THE ENRAGED

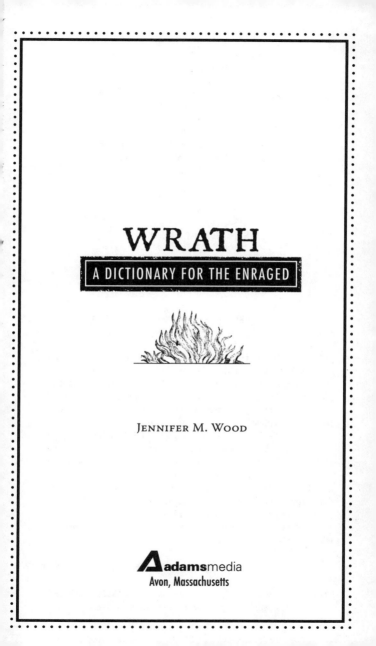

JENNIFER M. WOOD

Aadamsmedia
Avon, Massachusetts

Published by
Adams Media, a division of F+W Media, Inc.
57 Littlefield Street, Avon, MA 02322. U.S.A.
www.adamsmedia.com

ISBN 10: 1-4405-2803-9
ISBN 13: 978-1-4405-2803-3
eISBN 10: 1-4405-2829-2
eISBN 13: 978-1-4405-2829-3

Printed in the United States of America.

10   9   8   7   6   5   4   3   2   1

Library of Congress Cataloging-in-Publication Data
is available from the publisher.

This publication is designed to provide accurate and authoritative information with regard to the subject matter covered. It is sold with the understanding that the publisher is not engaged in rendering legal, accounting, or other professional advice. If legal advice or other expert assistance is required, the services of a competent professional person should be sought.

—From a *Declaration of Principles* jointly adopted
by a Committee of the American Bar Association
and a Committee of Publishers and Associations

Many of the designations used by manufacturers and sellers to distinguish their product are claimed as trademarks. Where those designations appear in this book and Adams Media was aware of a trademark claim, the designations have been printed with initial capital letters.

Fire image © clipart.com

*This book is available at quantity discounts for bulk purchases.
For information, please call 1-800-289-0963.*

An Introduction to
Wrath

wrath
(*rath*)

NOUN: An intense anger; a vengeful punishment.

Many sins sow the seeds for war, but the unmitigated rage responsible for its execution comes from wrath. The destruction, the loss, the pain—all are left in the wake of this particular sin. Whether it comes down from on high like the gods' rage in Homer's *Odyssey* or boils up from inside like the fuel of Ahab's vengeful voyage, the vice's choking grip has been felt throughout history and literature. Sometimes justified, oftentimes not, the results are always the same. While wrath is best defined in the gritted teeth and white-knuckled fist of the enraged, this short dictionary captures the spirit of the most combative sin.

A

abash

(*uh-BASH*)

VERB: To humiliate, shame, or embarrass someone.

abhorrent

(*ab-HOR-ent*)

ADJECTIVE: Repulsive or reprehensible.

abominate

(*uh-BOM-ih-nayt*)

VERB: To detest or hate intensely.

> *Even though the divorce was finalized, it didn't change the fact that Rachel still ABOMINATED her ex-husband for having an affair.*

acerbate

(*AS-er-bayt*)

VERB OR ADJECTIVE: As a verb, to exasperate. As an adjective, embittered.

acrid

(*AK-rid*)

ADJECTIVE: Most often used to describe something that is bitter or harsh in smell or taste, the word can be applied in a more general sense to anything that is extremely angry and bitter.

acrimonious

(*ak-ri-MO-nee-us*)

ADJECTIVE: Bitter or hostile; something that is acrimonious is filled with anger and animosity.

adverse

(*AD-vers*)

ADJECTIVE: Acting in opposition to or in an antagonistic manner; unfavorable; hostile.

affliction

(*uh-FLICK-shun*)

NOUN: A condition of physical or mental suffering; hardship.

> *Sophie's self-hatred became such an AFFLICTION that no one was surprised by her eventual suicide.*

aggravate

(*AG-ruh-vayt*)

VERB: to make worse; to intensify; to cause to become irritated or inflamed.

alienate

(*AY-lee-uh-nayt*)

VERB: To isolate or make someone feel as if he or she no longer belongs somewhere; estrange.

amerce
(*uh-MERSS*)
VERB: To punish, especially with a monetary fine.

anathema
(*uh-NATH-eh-muh*)
NOUN: A person or thing that is shunned because it is extremely disliked or loathsome.

anger
(*ANG-ger*)
NOUN OR VERB: As a noun, a strong feeling of displeasure. As a verb, to arouse wrath within.

animadversion
(*an-uh-mad-VER-zhun*)
NOUN: An extremely critical and reproachful comment.

animosity
(*an-ih-MOSS-ih-tee*)
NOUN: Extreme hostility or resentment.

animus
(*AN-uh-muss*)
NOUN: Hostility or ill feeling.

I was angry with my friend:

I told my wrath,

my wrath did end.

I was angry with my foe:

I told it not,

my wrath did grow.

—WILLIAM BLAKE

antagonism

(*an-TAG-uh-niz-uhm*)

NOUN: An opposition between unfriendly or conflicting people or groups.

antipathy

(*an-TIP-uh-thee*)

NOUN: A feeling of strong revulsion or hostility or the source of that hostility.

If you feel such ANTIPATHY towards your job, why do you continue to go?

apocalyptic

(*uh-pok-uh-LIP-tik*)

ADJECTIVE: As in the Bible's book of Revelation, apocalyptic refers to an event involving widespread destruction or disaster.

apoplectic

(*ap-uh-PLECK-tic*)

ADJECTIVE: An "apoplexy" is a stroke, so apoplectic can refer to the symptoms of a stroke, but it also refers to being in a state of extreme anger or rage.

arson

(*AHR-suhn*)

NOUN: The intentional destruction of property by fire for malicious reasons.

artifice

(*ART-ih-fuss*)

NOUN: Clever trickery or deceit.

> *Through your well-rehearsed ARTIFICE you were able to embezzle over $40,000.*

askance

(*uh-SKANTS*)

ADVERB: Can refer to looking at something in a sideways manner or with suspicion or disapproval; doubtfully.

asperity

(*a-SPAYR-ih-tee*)

NOUN: A manner that is harsh or severe; brusqueness.

aspersion

(*uh-SPUR-zhun*)

NOUN: A slanderous or defamatory charge; false accusation. The word is often used in the plural.

aversion

(*uh-VUR-zhun*)

NOUN: Extreme hatred or loathing; repugnance.

B

baleful

(*BAYL-ful*)

ADJECTIVE: Threatening misfortune to come; ominous.

bane

(*bayn*)

NOUN: Something that causes harm or destruction; scourge.

barbarism

(*BAR-ber-ism*)

NOUN: Uncivilized or brutal behavior or actions; savagery.

bedlam

(*BED-lum*)

NOUN: A situation marked by confusion or chaos; mayhem.

> *During the riots out in the streets, the BEDLAM was such that we were unable to get in or out of our flat.*

belabor

(*bih-LAY-burr*)

VERB: To attack or assault either physically or verbally.

beleaguer
(*bee-LEEG-urr*)
VERB: To besiege or harass a person; bother.

belligerent
(*buh-LIJ-er-ent*)
ADJECTIVE: From the Latin word for "war," a belligerent person is someone who is argumentative or pugnacious.

bemoan
(*bih-MOAN*)
VERB: To express regret or disappointment; lament.

> *Never one to be content, Isabel was always the first to BEMOAN the restaurant choice.*

besiege
(*bih-SEEJ*)
VERB: To surround a person or group in an attempt to capture it; to harass or overwhelm.

bestial
(*BESS-chul*)
ADJECTIVE: Beastly or inhuman; savage or brutal.

Anger and jealousy can no

more bear to lose sight of

their objects than love.

—George Eliot

bête noire

(*bett NWAHR*)

NOUN: French for "black beast," *bête noire* is an extremely disliked or frightening person or thing.

(*BILL-yes*)

ADJECTIVE: Related to the word "bile," *bilious* refers to a thing or person that is unsettling or irritable; bad-tempered.

blacklist

(*BLAK-list*)

VERB: To shun a person because his or her behavior goes against something that is considered right or moral.

bludgeon

(*BLUD-jun*)

VERB: To beat someone repeatedly with an object. As a noun, a *bludgeon* is a club that can be used as a weapon.

bluster

(*BLUS-ter*)

VERB: To behave in a loud, obnoxious way or in a manner that could threaten someone; harangue.

> *Not normally one to BLUSTER, it was surprising when Timothy yelled offensive statements out of the window.*

boil

(*boyl*)

VERB: Most commonly used in reference to the point where a liquid becomes a gas, to boil also means to seethe with anger; fume.

bombard

(*bom-BARD*)

VERB: To place under attack; assail.

bout

(*bowt*)

NOUN: A short period of time spent doing something, like a bout with the flu, or a contest or fight.

brandish

(*BRAN-dish*)

VERB: To show something in a menacing way; wield.

Annabel will BRANDISH the knife to her husband, whether or not she intends to use it, if he threatens her again.

brash

(*brash*)

ADJECTIVE: Impetuous or hasty; aggressive.

brazen

(*BRAY-zun*)

ADJECTIVE: Bold or brash; shameless. The adverb form is brazenly.

brouhaha

(*BROO-ha-ha*)

NOUN: An event marked by noise or conflict; a commotion or ruckus.

brunt

(*brunt*)

NOUN: The primary force or impact of something, as in an attack.

brusque

(*brusk*)

ADJECTIVE: An abrupt or short manner; curt.

bugaboo

(*BUG-uh-boo*)

NOUN: A person or thing that causes obsessive fear or anxiety; a persistent problem.

The dark figure on the corner of my street causes such a BUGABOO that the other neighbors and I have taken to walking the long way home.

Control thy passions,

lest they take vengeance

on thee.

—Epictetus

bull
(*bull*)

VERB: To push or drive powerfully or violently.

bumptious
(*BUMP-shuss*)

ADJECTIVE: Overbearing and self-important; pushy.

I'm tired of Peter being so BUMPTIOUS toward his wife; she is never able to make any decisions or even speak without being interrupted.

C

calamity
(*kuh-LAMM-ih-tee*)
NOUN: An event causing great misfortune or disaster; misery that results from a disaster.

callous
(*KAL-uss*)
ADJECTIVE: Unconcerned about others' feelings; heartless.

calumny
(*KAL-um-nee*)
NOUN: A false or slanderous statement made with malicious intent; defamation.

canard
(*kuh-NARD*)
NOUN: A false accusation or fabrication; a rumor.

It was cruel of Colette to invent such a CANARD about her sister, especially considering how many others she told.

cantankerous
(*kan-TANG-ker-us*)
ADJECTIVE: Argumentative or irritable.

captious

(*KAP-shuss*)

ADJECTIVE: Describes a person who is extremely critical and often finds fault with others for trivial matters.

carp

(*karp*)

VERB: To complain loudly and excessively, particularly about trivial matters.

> *There is no need to continue to CARP about your dislike for tonight's dinner; tomorrow night you can prepare your own.*

castigate

(*KASS-tuh-gate*)

VERB: To reprimand or punish severely; criticize.

cataclysm

(*kat-uh-KLIZZ-uhm*)

NOUN: A sudden and destructive change or upheaval; a catastrophe.

caustic

(*KOSS-tick*)

ADJECTIVE: Biting or particularly sarcastic; scathing.

cavil

(*KAV-ihl*)

VERB: To complain or split hairs regarding trivial matters.

censorious

(*sen-SOR-ee-us*)

ADJECTIVE: Extremely disapproving or critical; stern.

censure

(*SEN-sher*)

VERB: To fault or disapprove of something; criticize. As a noun, the word refers to extreme criticism.

chafe

(*chayf*)

VERB: To rub or cause friction; to irritate or annoy.

chagrin

(*shuh-GRIN*)

NOUN: Feeling humiliated or mortified as a result of an embarrassing situation.

> *Though it gave her much CHAGRIN, Petra held her head high and walked through the crowd with half of her dress missing.*

He enter'd,

but he enter'd full of wrath.

—JOHN KEATS

chide
(*chyd*)
VERB: To scold or reprimand someone; reproach.

choler
(*KAHL-er*)
NOUN: Anger or irritability.

clamor
(*KLAM-uhr*)
NOUN: A loud uproar or disturbance; upheaval.

clout
(*klowt*)
NOUN: The influence or importance a person or thing holds; as a verb, it means to hit somebody with one's hand.

collude
(*kuh-LOOD*)
VERB: To conspire or scheme with someone for the purpose of doing something illegal.

Tonight we will COLLUDE with the other thieves in preparation for tomorrow's heist.

complicit
(*kum-PLIS-it*)
ADJECTIVE: To be involved in something illicit.

contemptuous

(*kun-TEMP-choo-us*)

ADJECTIVE: Expressing disdain or disapproval; scornful.

contentious

(*kuhn-TEN-chuss*)

ADJECTIVE: Having a tendency to disagree or fight; argumentative.

> *Our marriage has become increasingly CONTENTIOUS; it seems we can no longer go a day without an argument.*

contravene

(*kon-truh-VEEN*)

VERB: To disobey or break a rule.

contrive

(*kun-TRYV*)

VERB: To plot or scheme; to accomplish something by being clever.

controvert

(*KON-truh-VERT*)

VERB: To strongly oppose something; refute.

In battling evil, excess is good; for he who is moderate in announcing the truth is presenting half-truth. He conceals the other half out of fear of other people's wrath.

—Kahlil Gibran

contumely

(*kon-TYOO-muh-lee*)

NOUN: Insulting or contemptuous behavior or language arising from arrogance.

coup de grâce

(*koo duh GRAHS*)

NOUN: The final event or stroke that brings a situation to a conclusion; a death blow.

> *Most believe it was the suspicion of sorcery that was the COUP DE GRÂCE for Mary's beheading, but others feel it was long in coming.*

culpability

(*kul-puh-BILL-ih-tee*)

NOUN: Accountability or responsibility for some sort of wrongdoing.

D

dander

(*DAN-der*)

NOUN: Anger or bad humor.

dauntless

(*DAWNT-luss*)

ADJECTIVE: Unable to be frightened or intimidated; fearless.

> *Years of crime and abuse made him DAUNTLESS; even backed into a corner and outnumbered, he was not afraid.*

deadlock

(*DED-lok*)

NOUN: A standstill that occurs when two opposing forces can no longer progress any further in a dispute; impasse.

debacle

(*dih-BA-kull*)

NOUN: A disaster or catastrophe; an absolute fiasco.

debase

(*dih-BAYS*)

VERB: To reduce in value or status.

decry

(*dih-CRY*)

VERB: To criticize or condemn; belittle.

deface

(*dih-FAYS*)

VERB: To ruin or damage the appearance of something; soil.

defamation

(*def-uh-MAY-shun*)

NOUN: An unfounded attack on someone's reputation; slander.

> *You must apologize to Irene for announcing her misdeeds to the public; such DEFAMATION was not warranted.*

defenestration

(*dee-FEN-uh-STRAY-shun*)

NOUN: The act of throwing an object or person out of a window.

deign

(*dayn*)

VERB: To condescend or demean oneself; to stoop.

deleterious

(*del-ih-TEER-ee-us*)

ADJECTIVE: An effect that is harmful or damaging.

delusion

(*de-LOO-zhun*)

NOUN: A false illusion or belief; fallacy.

Even with your success as a model, your extreme self-loathing has you under the DELUSION that you are not beautiful.

denigrate

(*DEN-ih-grayt*)

VERB: To disparage one's character or reputation; defame.

denounce

(*dih-NOWNTS*)

VERB: To criticize harshly; condemn.

deplorable

(*de-PLOHR-uh-bull*)

ADJECTIVE: Wretched or dreadful.

depose

(*dih-POHZ*)

VERB: To remove someone from a position of authority. In a legal sense, it means to record the testimony of someone who is under oath.

depraved

(*duh-PRAYVD*)

ADJECTIVE: Immoral or wicked; degenerate.

depravity

(*dih-PRAV-ih-tee*)

NOUN: A state of corruption or immorality; wickedness.

deprecate

(*DEP-rih-kate*)

VERB: To condemn or belittle a person, thing, or idea; criticize.

derange

(*dih-RAYNJ*)

VERB: To throw into disorder; to disturb the condition of; to make insane.

deride

(*dih-RYD*)

VERB: To ridicule or mock someone with malicious intent; disparage.

derision

(*de-RIZH-un*)

NOUN: Scorn or contempt for a person, thing, or idea.

> *Her unfounded DERISION for cultures other than her own made traveling to foreign countries loathsome.*

derogatory

(*dih-ROG-uh-tore-ee*)

ADJECTIVE: Insulting or offensive; disparaging.

desecrate

(*DESS-ih-krayt*)

VERB: To damage or destroy something sacred; defile.

despotism

(*DESS-po-tiz-um*)

NOUN: Authoritarian rule. *Despotism* is a system where one dominant figure exercises complete power.

> *Since Hitler's DESPOTISM, Germans have been wary of authority figures emerging from nowhere and gaining power quickly.*

détente

(*DAY-tahnt*)

NOUN: From the French word meaning "to slacken," *détente* is a reduction of hostility in a strained relationship.

detrimental

(*det-rih-MEN-tul*)

ADJECTIVE: Having a damaging or harmful effect.

diabolical

(*dye-uh-BOL-ih-kul*)

ADJECTIVE: Stemming from the word for "devil," something that is *diabolical* is wicked or evil.

diatribe

(*DY-uh-tryb*)

NOUN: An abusive verbal or written attack against a person or idea.

dichotomy

(*dy-KOT-uh-mee*)

NOUN: The division of two contrasting parts or ideas.

disabuse

(*diss-uh-BYOOZ*)

VERB: To realize or force someone else to realize that an incorrect notion is, in fact, incorrect.

disapprobation

(*dis-ap-ruh-BAY-shuhn*)

NOUN: Disapproval; moral condemnation.

discombobulate

(*diss-kum-BOB-yoo-layt*)

VERB: To confuse or disconcert.

> *It is easy to DISCOMBOBULATE your blind sister by rearranging the furniture.*

discomfit

(*diss-KUM-fit*)

VERB: To confuse or embarrass someone; to frustrate one's plans.

discomfort

(*diss-KUM-fort*)

NOUN: Mental or bodily distress or unease.

disconsolate

(*dis-KON-suh-lut*)

ADJECTIVE: Incredibly unhappy, so much so that he or she is beyond consolation; melancholy.

Nor hell a fury

like a woman scorned.

—William Congreve

discordant

(*dis-KOR-dunt*)

ADJECTIVE: In disagreement with; conflicting.

> *You have told me two DISCORDANT versions of the same story, and I'm having trouble determining which is the truth.*

discrepancy

(*dis-KREP-un-see*)

NOUN: A difference between two things that should be the same; inconsistency.

disdain

(*diss-DAYN*)

NOUN: Extreme contempt or scorn; as a verb, it means to view someone with such contempt.

disgruntled

(*diss-GRUN-tulld*)

ADJECTIVE: Discontented or dissatisfied to the point of annoyance.

disingenuous

(*diss-in-JEN-yoo-uss*)

ADJECTIVE: Not genuine or truthful; insincere or calculating.

> *When you are DISINGENUOUS by lying about one topic, people are less inclined to trust you in other topics.*

disparage
(*diss-PAYR-udge*)
VERB: To speak about someone in a belittling manner; defame or criticize.

dispel
(*dis-PELL*)
VERB: To dismiss an idea that is incorrect; disabuse.

displeasure
(*dis-PLEZH-er*)
NOUN OR VERB: As a noun, dissatisfaction; disapproval; annoyance; discomfort; uneasiness; pain. As a verb, to displease.

disputation
(*dis-pyoo-TAY-shun*)
NOUN: An argument or debate, particularly a formal one.

dissemble
(*diss-SEM-bul*)
VERB: To act in a disingenuous or misleading way; evade.

dissidence

(*DISS-uh-dents*)

NOUN: Disagreement, particularly with a widely held opinion or government.

dissuade

(*diss-SWAYD*)

NOUN: To convince someone not to act in a way that he or she had planned to; discourage.

distemper

(*dis-TEM-per*)

NOUN: A deranged condition of mind or body; a disorder; a disturbance.

distraught

(*dih-STRAWT*)

ADJECTIVE: Extremely upset or distressed; hysterical.

divulge

(*dih-VULJ*)

VERB: To make known something confidential or private.

dogged

(*DAW-gihd*)

ADJECTIVE: Utterly determined; relentless.

doleful

(*DOHL-full*)

ADJECTIVE: Extremely sad or unhappy; miserable.

I pitied Penelope; her DOLEFUL temperament left her weepy, dark, and listless most days, with no potential to be cheered up.

donnybrook

(*DAHN-ee-brook*)

NOUN: A wild dispute or brawl; fracas.

duplicity

(*doo-PLISS-ih-tee*)

NOUN: Deceptiveness or dishonesty.

duress

(*dur-ESS*)

NOUN: Constraint by threat; coercion.

dyspeptic

(*diss-PEP-tick*)

ADJECTIVE: Ill-tempered or irritable; acting as if one is suffering from dyspepsia, or indigestion.

dystopia

(*diss-TOHP-ee-uh*)

NOUN: The opposite of a utopia, a *dystopia* is an imagined place where everything is at its absolute worst.

After the constant bombing and subsequent adversarial occupation, the once beautiful city became a DYSTOPIA, the place of nightmares.

E

effrontery

(*ih-FRON-ter-ee*)

NOUN: Immense nerve; audacity.

egocentric

(*ee-go-SEN-trik*)

ADJECTIVE: Behaving as if you are the only person who matters; extremely self-centered.

emasculate

(*ee-MASS-kyoo-layt*)

VERB: To weaken someone's strength or power; castrate.

embroil

(*em-BROYL*)

VERB: To entangle someone in a conflict or situation.

> *Though Harold was not initially involved in the dispute, Thomas would later EMBROIL him into it in hopes of having someone on his side.*

enjoin

(*en-JOYN*)

VERB: To direct someone to do something or to prohibit someone from doing something.

enmesh

(*en-MESH*)

VERB: To embroil someone in a situation from which it is difficult to extricate oneself; entangle.

enmity

(*EN-mi-tee*)

NOUN: Shared hatred or hostility between two opposing forces or enemies.

eradicate

(*ee-RAD-ih-cayt*)

VERB: To completely eliminate or destroy something; exterminate.

estranged

(*ih-STREYNJD*)

ADJECTIVE: Alienated or separated.

evade

(*ee-VAYD*)

VERB: To avoid or dodge a person or thing, often by deception or trickery; elude.

> *You may have been able to EVADE your father up to this point by hiding at school, but eventually you will have to go home, where he will surely find you.*

If an injury has to be done to

a man, it should be so severe

that his vengeance need

not be feared.

—Niccolo Machiavelli

eviscerate

(*ee-VIS-uh-rayt*)

VERB: To disembowel; to remove a vital part of something.

exacerbate

(*ig-ZASS-ur-bayt*)

VERB: To aggravate an already existing problem; worsen.

excommunicate

(*eks-kuh-MYOO-nih-kayt*)

VERB: To formally banish or exclude someone from participating in a group.

excoriate

(*ik-SKORE-ee-ayt*)

VERB: To attack a person, thing, or idea harshly; berate.

> *George was EXCORIATED by the teacher in front of the class for not doing his homework.*

execrable

(*ek-ZEK-ruh-bul*)

ADJECTIVE: Appalling or disgusting.

expletive

(*EK-splih-tihv*)

NOUN: A profane exclamation or swear word.

exploit

(*eck-SPLOYT*)

VERB: To use a person or situation for personal gain or profit; to take advantage of a person or situation.

F

fabricate

(*FAB-rih-kayt*)

VERB: To manufacture something, including a story that is not true.

fabulist

(*FAB-yuh-list*)

NOUN: A person who tells outrageous lies.

She was such an incredible FABULIST that eventually no one believed anything she said at all.

fallacy

(*FALL-uh-see*)

NOUN: An erroneous notion; misconception.

farouche

(*fuh-ROOSH*)

ADJECTIVE: From the French word meaning "belonging outside," *farouche* is used to describe an unsociable or sullen person; menacing.

faux pas

(*foe PAH*)

NOUN: An embarrassing social error or gaffe.

faze

(*fayz*)

VERB: To bother or disturb somebody.

felonious

(*fuh-LOHN-ee-uss*)

ADJECTIVE: Pertaining to the behavior of a felon; criminal or villainous.

ferret

(*FER-it*)

VERB: To drive out by force, as if one were using ferrets.

ferule

(*FER-uhl*)

NOUN: A stick or piece of wood used to punish a child, typically by hitting them on the hand.

The nuns at the school were all equipped with a FERULE, which they would use to punish unruly children.

fetters

(*FET-urz*)

NOUN: Shackles, handcuffs, or some sort of restraint.

fiasco

(*fee-ASS-koe*)

NOUN: A complete failure or disaster; debacle.

filch

(*filch*)

VERB: To steal something, particularly a small amount or something very inexpensive.

finagle

(*fih-NAY-gul*)

VERB: To manipulate a person or situation—usually with trickery—in order to achieve a goal.

flagellate

(*FLADGE-uh-layt*)

VERB: To whip or flog a person or thing.

flagitious

(*fluh-JISH-us*)

ADJECTIVE: A person or situation that is particularly shameful or wicked; vicious.

> *No one had ever seen such a FLAGITIOUS little girl; with her violence and language they began to believe she was possessed by a demon.*

flagrant

(*FLAY-grunt*)

ADJECTIVE: Something that blatantly goes against typical conduct or standards.

flare up

(*flayr up*)

VERB: To burn, as a torch; to burst out in sudden, fierce activity or passion.

flashpoint

(*FLASH-point*)

NOUN: A place where violence is likely to occur, or has occurred in the past, often as a result of political tensions.

fleer

(*fleer*)

VERB: To smirk or laugh derisively. As a noun, a scathing look or comment; smirk.

flippant

(*FLIP-unt*)

ADJECTIVE: Disrespectful or dismissive; glib.

She was so FLIPPANT about her father's death that we suspected she knew about it before it happened.

flout

(*flowt*)

VERB: To break a law; to behave in a contemptible manner.

foist

(*foyst*)

VERB: To force an undesirable thing on someone; impose.

foolhardy

(*FOOL-har-dee*)

ADJECTIVE: Reckless or rash; making quick decisions but not using good sense.

forcible

(*FORSS-ih-bul*)

ADJECTIVE: Using aggressive or physical power to attain a goal.

formidable

(*FOR-mih-duh-bull*)

ADJECTIVE: A person or thing that quickly inspires fear or respect because of its strength and power.

forsake

(*for-SAYK*)

VERB: To abandon or renounce.

fracas

(*FRAK-us*)

NOUN: A noisy argument or quarrel; brawl.

> *By leaving the pub early, you avoided the violent FRACAS that later ensued between two men over one woman.*

Usually when people are sad,

they don't do anything. They

just cry over their condition.

But when they get angry,

they bring about a change.

—MALCOLM X

fractious
(*FRAK-shuss*)
ADJECTIVE: Prone to complaining and misbehavior; irritable.

fratricide
(*FRAT-rih-syd*)
NOUN: The act of killing one's brother.

fret
(*fret*)
VERB: To experience worry, annoyance, discontent; to torment; to wear away by gnawing.

fulminate
(*FUL-mih-nayt*)
VERB: To criticize harshly; to explode.

fume
(*fyoom*)
VERB: To seethe with extreme anger but not let all of it be known.

funereal
(*fyoo-NIR-ee-uhl*)
ADJECTIVE: Pertaining to a funeral; mournful or solemn.

furor

(*FYOOR-ur*)

NOUN: Intense anger or fury.

I had never witnessed such a FUROR as when he yelled and ran at you with the knife.

fury

(*FYOOR-ee*)

NOUN: Unrestrained or violent anger, rage, or passion; violence; vehemence. In classical mythology, the Furies pertain to minor female divinities who punished crimes at the instigation of the victims.

G

gadfly
(*GAD-fly*)
NOUN: Like a fly that attacks livestock, a *gadfly* is a person who constantly torments a person; pest.

gainsay
(*GAYN-say*)
VERB: To declare that something is false; oppose.

genocide
(*JENN-uh-syd*)
NOUN: The intentional destruction of an entire culture or nation.

glower
(*GLOU-ur*)
VERB: To glare at or give someone an annoyed, sullen look; scowl.

> *It was not unheard of for her to twist her face into a GLOWER when anyone offered helpful advice.*

gnash
(*nash*)
VERB: To grind one's teeth in anger or frustration.

Dangerous is wrath

concealed. Hatred

proclaimed doth lose

its chance of wreaking

vengeance.

—SENECA

goad
(*gohd*)
VERB: To annoy or provoke someone to take action.

grapple
(*GRAP-ul*)
VERB: To wrestle with an opponent or difficult situation; tackle.

You have to consider all of the consequences of each option while you GRAPPLE with this decision.

grimace
(*GRIM-uss*)
VERB: To scowl or show discomfort through one's facial expression; as a noun, it refers to the frown that one makes while grimacing.

grisly
(*GRIZ-lee*)
ADJECTIVE: Gruesome or horrific.

grouse
(*growss*)
VERB: To complain or grumble; moan.

grudge

(*gruhj*)

NOUN: An ongoing feeling of animosity or ill will.

guile

(*gyl*)

NOUN: Cunning or deceit; deviousness.

> *If not for her GUILE, she would not have been able to persuade her kidnapper to let her leave her imprisonment.*

H

harangue

(*huh-RANG*)

VERB: To berate or criticize in a forceful, angry way.

harrowing

(*HAYR-roe-ing*)

ADJECTIVE: Extremely disturbing or upsetting; distressing.

> *The details of his murder are especially HARROWING; what she did to his body required a great deal of strength and violence.*

harry

(*HAYR-ee*)

VERB: To harass or bother someone excessively; pester.

hateful

(*HAYT-ful*)

ADJECTIVE: Full of hate or spite; malevolent.

hector

(*HEK-ter*)

VERB: To bully or intimidate someone.

Revenge is sweet

but not nourishing.

—MASON COOLEY

heinous

(*HAY-nuss*)

ADJECTIVE: Wicked or reprehensible; atrocious.

histrionic

(*hiss-tree-ON-ihk*)

ADJECTIVE: Can relate to the dramatic behavior of an actor on stage or, more generally, describe real-life behavior that is overly theatrical or dramatic. It is sometimes used as a noun in the plural form: histrionics.

hotspur

(*HOT-spur*)

NOUN: From Shakespeare's *Henry IV*, a hotspur is an impetuous person; hothead.

hubbub

(*HUB-ub*)

NOUN: A commotion; an outburst.

With all the HUBBUB coming from the townspeople, it was no time at all before a mob was formed to kill him.

hubris

(*HYOO-briss*)

NOUN: *Hubris*, or excessive pride, was often the fatal flaw of many characters in Greek tragedies; narcissism.

huff

(*huff*)

NOUN: An instance or anger or resentment.

I

ignominious
(*ig-no-MIN-ee-uss*)
ADJECTIVE: Humiliating or disgraceful;
dishonorable.

ill will
(*ill will*)
NOUN: Animosity or hostility toward a person.

illicit
(*ih-LISS-it*)
ADJECTIVE: Illegal or unlawful; immoral.

imbroglio
(*im-BRO-lee-yo*)
NOUN: A complicated or confusing situation that is
marked by disagreement; mess.

immolation
(*IM-uh-LAY-shun*)
NOUN: To kill a person or animal as a sacrifice, par-
ticularly by fire.

immure
(*i-MYOOR*)
VERB: To imprison or confine someone.

> *If we did not IMMURE him in a cell all night, he
> would surely kill again.*

impale

(*im-PAYL*)

VERB: To pierce or stab a person or thing with a sharp object.

impede

(*im-PEED*)

VERB: To obstruct or interfere with one's progress; hinder.

impertinent

(*im-PURR-tih-nent*)

ADJECTIVE: Rude or disrespectful; insolent.

impetuous

(*im-PETCH-you-us*)

ADJECTIVE: Behaving in an impulsive or rash manner; hotheaded.

It was IMPETUOUS of her to run off without warning and join the circus.

impetus

(*IHM-puh-tuss*)

NOUN: Something that provides motivation; momentum.

implacable

(*im-PLACK-uh-bull*)

ADJECTIVE: Unable to be pacified; merciless.

impregnable

(*im-PREG-nuh-bull*)

ADJECTIVE: Something that is too strong to be captured or penetrated; unconquerable.

impropriety

(*im-pro-PRY-ih-tee*)

NOUN: Something that is contrary to normally accepted behavior; bad taste.

impugn

(*im-PYOON*)

VERB: To challenge the honesty or genuineness of a person or claim; censure.

Based on Eloise's outrageous and unbelievable account, it was necessary for the lawyer to IMPUGN her testimony for credibility.

incarcerate

(*in-KAHR-suh-rayt*)

VERB: To imprison somebody.

incense

(*in-SENS*)

VERB: To enrage or infuriate someone.

inculpate

(*in-KUL-payt*)

VERB: To incriminate or blame somebody for something.

> *Even though the lie would INCULPATE her brother in her father's murder, she felt it was necessary to protect herself.*

indict

(*in-DYT*)

VERB: To formally accuse or charge someone with a crime.

indignant

(*in-DIG-nunt*)

ADJECTIVE: Angry or offended by unfair behavior; resentful.

inexorable

(*in-EK-sur-uh-bul*)

ADJECTIVE: Unable to be persuaded or moved; unstoppable.

Not by wrath, but by

laughter do we kill.

Come, let us kill

the spirit of gravity!

—Friedrich Nietzsche

infamous

(*IN-fun-muhs*)

ADJECTIVE: Well-known because of a bad reputation; notorious.

infernal

(*in-FER-nul*)

ADJECTIVE: Literally translated, something that is *infernal* is "of or pertaining to hell." It is used to describe something wicked or devilish.

infuriate

(*in-FYOOR-ee-ayt*)

VERB: To make extremely angry; enrage.

inimical

(*in-IM-ih-kul*)

ADJECTIVE: Injurious or harmful; detrimental.

iniquity

(*ih-NIK-wih-tee*)

NOUN: From the Latin phrase for "unfair," *iniquity* refers to an unjust or immoral act.

insensate

(*in-SENS-ayt*)

ADJECTIVE: Lacking feeling or common sense; anesthetized.

> *Because the killings were so gruesome and heartless, the killer was most likely INSENSATE.*

insidious

(*in-SID-ee-uss*)

ADJECTIVE: Subtly menacing; dangerous.

insubordinate

(*in-suh-BOR-din-it*)

ADJECTIVE: Disobedient to authority or the accepted rules; defiant.

insular

(*IN-suh-ler*)

ADJECTIVE: Detached; self-centered or egocentric. An insult used to refer to a person who stands alone in his or her attitudes toward politics, religion, or moral ideas.

insuperable

(*in-SOO-pur-uh-bul*)

ADJECTIVE: Unable to be overcome; insurmountable.

> *The evidence against her is INSUPERABLE; there's no way to disprove her guilt.*

insurgence

(*in-SUR-junce*)

NOUN: An uprising against authority; revolt.

intractable

(*in-TRACK-tuh-bull*)

ADJECTIVE: Stubborn; inflexible; difficult to manage.

intransigent

(*in-TRAN-si-junt*)

ADJECTIVE: Unwilling to compromise or relent; inflexible.

If you weren't so INTRANSIGENT, you might be more open-minded to my arguments on the matter.

inure

(*in-YOOR*)

VERB: To habituate someone to an unpleasant thing to make it less unpleasant.

invective

(*in-VEK-tiv*)

NOUN: Insulting or abusive language; diatribe.

To take revenge

halfheartedly is to court

disaster: Either condemn or

crown your hatred.

—Pierre Corneille

inveigh

(*in-VAY*)

VERB: To speak against something strongly; condemn (usually followed by against).

invidious

(*in-VID-ee-uss*)

ADJECTIVE: Resulting in resentment or hatred; odious.

irascible

(*ih-RASS-uh-bul*)

ADJECTIVE: Prone to anger or petulance; irritable.

irate

(*aye-RAYT*)

ADJECTIVE: Furious; incredibly angry.

ire

(*ayer*)

NOUN: Extreme anger or rage.

> *It was his untamable IRE that caused the situation to elevate quickly and disproportionately.*

J and K

jail

(*jayl*)

NOUN: A prison intended for the detention of criminals, including murderers.

jealous

(*JEL-uhs*)

ADJECTIVE: Feeling anger or resentment against someone because of that person's advantages.

jeapordize

(*JEP-ur-dyz*)

VERB: To put someone in danger or in harm's way; endanger.

jinx

(*jingks*)

NOUN OR VERB: As a noun, a person, thing, or power meant to bring bad luck. As a verb, to bring bad luck to; to place a *jinx* on; to destroy the purpose of.

juggernaut

(*JUG-ur-not*)

NOUN: A powerful force that destroys everything in its path.

Beware the fury

of a patient man.

—JOHN DRYDEN

kill
(*kil*)

VERB: To destroy; to do away with; to extinguish; to cause the death of; to slay.

kill-joy
(*KIL-joi*)

NOUN: A person who spoils the happiness or pleasure of others.

knout
(*nout*)

NOUN: A leather whip used to flog a person or animal.

L

laceration

(*LASS-uh-RAY-shun*)

NOUN: A cut or tear.

> *The whip left a LACERATION across his back that required stitches.*

lachrymose

(*LAK-rih-mohs*)

ADJECTIVE: Characterized by weeping or tending to cause tears; mournful.

lambaste

(*lam-BAYST*)

VERB: To severely criticize someone; deride.

libel

(*LY-bull*)

NOUN: A false written or published statement made about someone that serves to damage his or her reputation—perhaps irreparably.

> *He lost his job at the paper for the LIBEL he allowed to go to press, proclaiming the governor was a fraud.*

litigious

(*lih-TIJ-us*)

ADJECTIVE: A person or organization that frequently files and engages in lawsuits.

Detestable flatterers!

The most deadly gift that

divine wrath may give a king!

—Jean Racine

livid
(*LIH-vid*)
ADJECTIVE: Furious.

loathe
(*loath*)
VERB: To detest or dislike a person or thing vehemently; hate.

louche
(*loosh*)
ADJECTIVE: Of questionable taste or morality; decadent.

> *He was LOUCHE in that he allowed the food to be served on the backs of the servants themselves rather than plates.*

lour
(*LOW-er*)
VERB: To frown or scowl.

machination

(*mak-uh-NAY-shun*)

NOUN: A scheme or plot, especially one devised to achieve an illicit goal.

> *The MACHINATION for this bank heist is becoming more and more complicated, and each person plays a vital role in order for us to succeed.*

madden

(*MAD-den*)

VERB: To make angry; enrage.

maelstrom

(*MAYL-strum*)

NOUN: A violent, confused situation that often results in destruction.

malcontent

(*MAL-kuhn-tent*)

NOUN: One who is not content with the current status of his or her life; can also be used as an adjective to describe someone who is dissatisfied.

maleficence

(*muh-LEF-ih-sence*)

NOUN: The act of doing harm or creating evil.

> *Your MALFEASANCE has not gone unnoticed; you will be punished accordingly when your father gets home.*

malevolent
(*muh-LEV-uh-lent*)
ADJECTIVE: Characterized by a desire to do harm to others; malicious.

malfeasance
(*mal-FEE-zunce*)
NOUN: Behavior that is marked by illegality or wrongdoing; misconduct.

malice
(*MAL-iss*)
NOUN: The intention or desire to do harm to others; spite.

malicious
(*muh-LISH-uss*)
ADJECTIVE: Spitefully mean; evil; bad in intent.

malign
(*muh-LYN*)
VERB: To sully the reputation of a person or thing, particularly by claiming information that is not true.

malignant
(*muh-LIG-nunt*)
ADJECTIVE: Liable to cause harm; hateful.

Come not between the

dragon and his wrath.

—WILLIAM SHAKESPEARE

mar

(*mar*)

VERB: To damage or spoil something; blight.

matricide

(*MAT-ruh-side*)

NOUN: The act of killing one's mother.

melee

(*MAY-lay*)

NOUN: A noisy confrontation between several people, most often in a public place; skirmish.

miasma

(*my-AS-muh*)

NOUN: A toxic atmosphere.

> *I am tired of living in this MIASMA day after day; I think it is making me sick.*

miff

(*mif*)

VERB: To irritate or anger somebody.

minatory

(*MIN-uh-tohr-ee*)

ADJECTIVE: Menacing or ominous.

misanthrope

(*MISS-un-throhp*)

NOUN: A person who hates all humankind.

miscreant

(*MISS-cree-uhnt*)

NOUN: A villain or evildoer.

> *He showed us what a true MISCREANT he was when he cut the orphans' portions in half to save money.*

misery

(*MIZ-uh-ree*)

NOUN: Extreme suffering or unhappiness; gloom.

mortify

(*MOHR-tih-fy*)

VERB: To humiliate or shame a person; embarrass.

N

nefarious

(*nih-FAYR-ee-uss*)

ADJECTIVE: Extremely evil; despicable.

It was unbelievably NEFARIOUS for her to drown the crying infant.

nemesis

(*NEM-ih-sis*)

NOUN: An enemy or opponent who seeks to exact revenge.

nettle

(*NET-l*)

VERB: To annoy or irritate; exasperate.

nocuous

(*NOK-yoo-uhs*)

ADJECTIVE: Liable to cause harm or injury; noxious.

noisome

(*NOI-suhm*)

ADJECTIVE: Offensive to the senses; harmful.

notoriety

(*noh-tuh-RY-uh-tee*)

NOUN: Infamy or ill repute; disrepute.

There is little for the great

part of the history of the

world except the bitter tears

of pity and the hot tears

of wrath.

—Woodrow Wilson

noxious
(*NOK-shuss*)
ADJECTIVE: Toxic or poisonous; harmful.

nuisance
(*NOO-suhns*)
NOUN: An annoying person or thing; pest.

obdurate

(*AHB-dur-uht*)

ADJECTIVE: Extremely stubborn or obstinate.

> *He wrapped his ankles around the chair and refused to leave, a display of his OBDURATE ways.*

objectionable

(*uhb-JEK-shun-uh-buhl*)

ADJECTIVE: Something that causes offense or opposition; disagreeable.

objurgate

(*OB-jur-gayt*)

VERB: To strongly berate or reprimand; renounce.

obloquy

(*OB-luh-kwee*)

NOUN: Abusive statements made against someone; denunciation.

obstinate

(*OB-stih-nut*)

ADJECTIVE: Unwilling to change an opinion or be swayed; stubborn.

Before you embark on

a journey of revenge,

dig two graves.

—CONFUCIUS

obstreperous

(*ob-STREP-er-us*)

ADJECTIVE: Extremely aggressive or hostile; defiant.

When any of the patients became OBSTREPEROUS, it was necessary for an orderly to restrain them and inject them with a tranquilizer.

odium

(*OH-dee-uhm*)

NOUN: Intense hatred or revulsion; abhorrence.

offend

(*uh-FEND*)

VERB: To insult someone or hurt his or her feelings.

ogre

(*OH-gur*)

NOUN: In a fairytale, an *ogre* is a man-eating monster; the term can also refer to a particularly unpleasant or wicked person.

ominous

(*OM-ih-nuss*)

ADJECTIVE: Suggesting possible harm or threat; foreboding.

opprobrium

(*uh-PRO-bree-um*)

NOUN: The disgrace that results from a disgraceful action.

> *After eating the cake off of the floor, Terrence had to deal with the OPPROBRIUM that followed from those that witnessed the act.*

ordnance

(*ORD-nunce*)

NOUN: Weaponry.

ostracize

(*OSS-truh-syz*)

VERB: To shun or banish someone.

outburst

(*OUT-burst*)

NOUN: A sudden burst or outbreak of emotion.

outrage

(*OUT-rayj*)

NOUN: Utter indignation or offense.

P

pandemonium

(*pan-duh-MOAN-ee-um*)

NOUN: A state of chaos or bedlam.

pander

(*PAN-der*)

VERB: To indulge or appeal to one's worst characteristics or base instincts.

paroxysm

(*PAYR-uk-siz-um*)

NOUN: A sudden outburst.

After months of silence, her startling PAROXYSM frightened everyone.

parricide

(*PAR-uh-syd*)

NOUN: The act of murdering one's parent or family member.

peeve

(*peev*)

VERB: To annoy or irritate; as a noun, *peeve* refers to something that annoys or irritates someone.

Anger as soon as fed is dead.

'Tis starving makes it fat.

—EMILY DICKINSON

pejorative

(*puh-JOHR-uh-tiv*)

ADJECTIVE: Critical or derogatory.

peremptory

(*puh-REMP-tuh-ree*)

ADJECTIVE: Something that is decisive and not open for further discussion; absolute.

> *After your unpredictable and violent tantrums, these restraints are PEREMPTORY until you calm down.*

perfidious

(*purr-FID-ee-uhs*)

ADJECTIVE: Deceitful or disloyal; treacherous.

pernicious

(*purr-NISH-uss*)

ADJECTIVE: Intending to cause harm or injury; destructive.

pertinacious

(*per-tih-NAY-shuss*)

ADJECTIVE: Annoyingly persistent; unshakable.

perturbation

(*pur-ter-BEY-shuhn*)

NOUN: A state of annoyance or agitation.

pest
(*pest*)
NOUN: A person or thing that is annoying; a nuisance.

pettifog
(*PET-ee-fawg*)
VERB: To argue about trivial matters; squabble.

petulant
(*PECH-oo-luhnt*)
ADJECTIVE: Sullen, irritable, or bad-tempered.

The PETULANT girl would sulk in her room for hours and then snap at the first person who greeted her once she emerged.

pique
(*peek*)
NOUN: A feeling of annoyance or exasperation; as a verb, to *pique* means to arouse one's interest or anger.

plague
(*playg*)
VERB: To torment; pester.

plaintive
(*PLAYN-tihv*)
ADJECTIVE: Mournful or sad.

plight
(*plyt*)
NOUN: A dangerous or desperate dilemma or predicament.

> *Sylvia felt that her PLIGHT of being unemployed with children to feed and a husband that gambled away all of his income justified his murder.*

polarize
(*PO-luh-rize*)
VERB: To further highlight two opposing sides; to pull apart.

polemic
(*puh-LEM-ik*)
NOUN: A strong verbal or written attack on an opinion or doctrine.

procrustean
(*pro-KRUS-tee-un*)
ADJECTIVE: Enforcing conformity by violent means.

provocateur
(*pro-vock-uh-TURR*)
NOUN: A person who intentionally provokes or stirs up trouble.

provocation

(*prov-uh-KAY-shuhn*)

NOUN: The act of intentionally provoking or aggravating a person or situation.

pugilist

(*PYOO-juh-lizt*)

NOUN: A boxer or fighter.

pugnacious

(*pug-NAY-shuss*)

ADJECTIVE: Inclined to aggression or fighting; confrontational.

The PUGNACIOUS wife picked fights with her husband and children, looking for confrontation wherever she could find it.

punishment

(*PUHN-ish-ment*)

NOUN: To inflict a sentence or penalty as a result of bad behavior.

putrid

(*PYOO-trid*)

ADJECTIVE: Disgusting or rotten, either physically or morally.

The only justice is to follow
the sincere intuition of the
soul, angry or gentle. Anger
is just, and pity is just, but
judgment is never just.

—D. H. LAWRENCE

quagmire
(*KWAG-myr*)
NOUN: An awkward predicament or entanglement.

quarrelsome
(*KWAR-uhl-sum*)
ADJECTIVE: Prone to argumentativeness;
cantankerous.

querulous
(*KWER-uh-luss*)
ADJECTIVE: Constantly complaining; grouchy.

> *You've been so QUERULOUS on this trip; I haven't
> heard anything from you except complaints.*

quibble
(*KWIB-uhl*)
VERB: To criticize or complain about trivial things;
bicker.

R

rage
(*rayj*)
NOUN: A fit or outburst of extreme anger or violence.

ramification
(*ram-ih-fih-KAY-shun*)
NOUN: The consequence of an action or decision.

rampage
(*RAM-payg*)
NOUN: An instance of uncontrolled violence.

rancor
(*RAN-kur*)
NOUN: Bitterness or ill will.

> *He had such RANCOR towards his ex-wife that when she brought the children to see him, he said horrible things about her to them.*

rankle
(*RANG-kul*)
VERB: To irritate or annoy; needle.

rant
(*rant*)

VERB: To shout or complain loudly; as a noun, a *rant* is the loud speech or complaining that a person does.

ravage
(*RAV-ij*)

VERB: To devastate or destroy something.

raze
(*rayz*)

VERB: To demolish or annihilate.

rebuke
(*rih-BYOOK*)

VERB: To harshly criticize or reprimand.

> *Your father thinks it is helpful to REBUKE you for your mistakes instead of offer you constructive criticism.*

recalcitrant
(*ri-KAL-sih-trunt*)

ADJECTIVE: Disobedient toward authority; obstinate.

Anger is a brief lunacy.

—Horace

relentless

(*ri-LENT-liss*)

ADJECTIVE: Pursuing a person or thing in a persistent, unyielding manner; unrelenting.

remonstrate

(*rih-MON-strayt*)

VERB: To forcefully protest or argue; oppose.

repercussion

(*ree-per-KUSH-un*)

NOUN: The consequence or result of an action or decision, sometimes one that is unforeseen or problematic.

reprehensible

(*rep-ri-HEN-sih-bull*)

ADJECTIVE: Repugnant or detestable.

reprisal

(*ree-PRAHY-zuhl*)

NOUN: A violent act of vengeance against a previous wrongdoing; retaliation.

reproach
(*ri-PROACH*)
VERB: To criticize someone for an incorrect or poor decision; admonish.

reprobate
(*REP-ruh-bayt*)
NOUN: A disreputable person; degenerate.

> *Do you think it was a wise idea to make a suspicious deal with such an unreliable REPROBATE?*

repugnant
(*ree-PUHG-nuhnt*)
ADJECTIVE: Revolting or repulsive; offensive.

repulse
(*ree-PUHLS*)
VERB: To completely offend; disgust.

requital
(*ri-KWAHYT-l*)
NOUN: Punishment or retaliation for some sort of wrongdoing.

restitution
(*res-ti-TOO-shun*)
NOUN: Compensation or repayment for a loss or injury; reimbursement.

restive

(*RES-tihv*)

ADJECTIVE: Impatient or restless.

retaliate

(*rih-TAL-ee-eyt*)

VERB: To harm someone in an attempt to even the score; to get even.

It was unnecessary to RETALIATE for your sister's beating; the police were taking care of it in a legal way.

retribution

(*re-truh-BYOO-shun*)

NOUN: Vengeance or punishment for a past wrongdoing.

revenge

(*rih-VENJ*)

NOUN: A punishment given in retaliation for something; vengeance.

revile

(*rih-VILE*)

VERB: To verbally abuse or attack someone; insult.

revulsion

(*rih-VUHL-shun*)

NOUN: A feeling of extreme disgust or loathing; repulsion.

rile

(*rayel*)

VERB: To annoy someone to the point of rage.

> *Don't RILE a person with your usual antics if he has a weapon in his hand.*

rival

(*RY-vuhl*)

NOUN: An adversary or opponent; as a verb, rival means to compete with someone.

ruckus

(*RUHK-uhs*)

NOUN: An unpleasant commotion; rumpus.

rue

(*roo*)

VERB: To regret or mourn.

> *She would RUE the decision to hire an assassin, but not until she was caught and punished for the crime.*

rumpus

(*RUM-puhs*)

NOUN: A loud commotion or disturbance.

sadistic

(*suh-DISS-tik*)

ADJECTIVE: Finding pleasure in inflicting violence or cruelty upon others; brutal.

sanguinary

(*SANG-gwuh-nayr-ee*)

ADJECTIVE: Pertaining to death or involving bloodshed.

sardonic

(*sar-DON-ik*)

ADJECTIVE: Extremely sarcastic or mocking; scornful.

> *That response to my emotional and heartfelt confession was SARDONIC and will not be taken seriously.*

saturnine

(*SAT-ur-neen*)

ADJECTIVE: Sluggish or morose.

savagery

(*SAV-ij-ree*)

NOUN: A state of being barbarous or uncivil; brutality.

scathing

(*SKAY-thing*)

ADJECTIVE: Extremely critical or contemptuous; derisive.

schadenfreude

(*SHAH-dun-froy-duh*)

NOUN: Finding pleasure in the misery or misfortune of others.

> *He seemed to derive such SCHADENFREUDE from cashing his generous paycheck in front of those begging for food.*

scourge

(*skuhrj*)

NOUN: A source of affliction or devastation; the word also refers to a whip used for punishment.

scurrilous

(*SKUR-ih-luss*)

ADJECTIVE: Verbally abusive or insulting; slanderous.

seethe

(*seeth*)

VERB: To remain in a state of unexpressed anger; fume.

shrew
(*shroo*)
NOUN: A violent or tempestuous woman.

shun
(*shun*)
VERB: To intentionally avoid or spurn a person, thing, or idea.

sinister
(*SIN-uh-ster*)
ADJECTIVE: Describes something that is menacing and has the potential for violence; evil.

skullduggery
(*skull-DUG-uh-ree*)
NOUN: Trickery or deceit; cheating.

> *I would be wary of playing cards with them; they're known for SKULLDUGGERY, and there are plenty of honest games to be found elsewhere.*

slander
(*SLAN-dur*)
VERB: To make a knowingly untrue statement or accusation against someone in an attempt to damage his or her reputation.

Life being what it is,

one dreams of revenge.

—Paul Gauguin

snit
(*snit*)
NOUN: An irritable state or bad mood.

solipsism
(*SOL-ip-siz-um*)
NOUN: The belief that the only thing that exists—or can be proven to exist—is oneself; self-absorption.

somber
(*SOM-ber*)
ADJECTIVE: Grave or depressing.

> *The SOMBER atmosphere of the funeral soon gave way to anger as many vowed to avenge his death.*

sophism
(*SOF-iz-uhm*)
NOUN: A flawed argument that is intentionally misleading or deceiving; fallacy.

sororicide
(*suh-RAHWR-uh-syd*)
NOUN: The act of killing one's sister.

spite
(*spyt*)
NOUN: Ill will toward a person or thing; malice.

spurn

(*spurn*)

VERB: To scornfully snub a person, thing, or idea; rebuff.

squabble

(*SKWOB-uhl*)

NOUN: A petty argument or quarrel; as a verb, it refers to the act of having such an argument.

squall

(*skwawl*)

NOUN: A brief commotion.

stigmatize

(*STIG-muh-tyz*)

VERB: To label a person, thing, or idea as evil or undesirable.

sully

(*SUL-ee*)

VERB: To pollute or spoil something, particularly one's reputation; vilify.

> *It would soon SULLY her reputation when people discovered how she sought such violent revenge on her ex-husband.*

surly

(*SUR-lee*)

ADJECTIVE: Ill-humored and gruff; rude.

T

tantrum
(*TAN-truhm*)
NOUN: A sudden or violent outburst of frustration or bad behavior.

tarnish
(*TAHR-nish*)
VERB: To destroy the purity of; to stain; to sully.

temerarious
(*tem-uh-RAIR-ee-uhs*)
ADJECTIVE: Reckless or impetuous.

temerity
(*tuh-MAYR-uh-tee*)
NOUN: Behavior that could be considered bold or rash; audacity.

temper
(*TEM-per*)
NOUN: Heat of mind or passion, often displayed in outbursts of anger or resentment.

tempest
(*TEM-pist*)
NOUN OR VERB: As a noun, a violent windstorm; a violent commotion; a disturbance; a tumult. As a verb, to disturb violently.

tempestuous

(*tem-PESS-choo-uss*)

ADJECTIVE: Prone to violence or extreme emotion; turbulent.

tenebrous

(*TEN-uh-bruhss*)

ADJECTIVE: Dark; ominous.

> *Genevieve watched over the hills as TENEBROUS clouds began forming; there would be a storm tonight.*

termagant

(*TER-muh-guhnt*)

NOUN: A violent, brawling woman; a shrew.

thrash

(*thrash*)

VERB: To beat soundly in punishment; to defeat thoroughly; to force.

tiff

(*tihf*)

NOUN: An argument or petty quarrel; a fit of annoyance; a bad mood; a spat, scrap, misunderstanding, or difference in opinions.

tirade

(*TIE-raid*)

NOUN: A verbal attack against a person, thing, or idea; outburst.

> *In her uninterrupted and very public TIRADE, she ranted about the government, her neighbors, and her marriage.*

torture

(*TAWR-cher*)

NOUN OR VERB: As a noun, the act of inflicting excruciating pain. As a verb, to subject to *torture*; to afflict with severe pain of body or mind; to force or extort; to punish.

traduce

(*truh-DOOSS*)

VERB: To knowingly make false accusations against a person; disparage.

trauma

(*TROU-muh*)

NOUN: A body wound caused by sudden injury whether intentionally violent or accidental in nature.

traumatize

(TRAW-muh-tyz)

VERB: To inflict psychological damage on someone; devastate.

troglodyte

(TROG-luh-dyt)

NOUN: A person who behaves in an uncivilized, beastly manner.

truculent

(TRUK-yuh-lunt)

ADJECTIVE: Prone toward hostility or defiance; argumentative.

tyrant

(TAY-runt)

NOUN: A ruler who uses abuses power; any person in a position of power who exercises power oppressively; a tyrannical influence.

In taking revenge, a man is

but even with his enemy;

but in passing it over, he is

superior.

—Sir Francis Bacon

U

umbrage
(*UM-brihj*)
NOUN: Resentment or offense.

unconscionable
(*un-KONSH-un-uh-bul*)
ADJECTIVE: Without conscience; immoral or unscrupulous.

underhanded
(*UN-dur-hand-id*)
ADJECTIVE: Sneaky or deceitful in nature; devious.

undermine
(*UN-dur-myn*)
VERB: To weaken something over time by chipping away at it, including a person's sense of self or importance.

> *Georgia found that it wasn't difficult to UNDERMINE her boss; with his soft-spoken voice, she was easily able to talk over him and change the plans he'd made.*

unsavory
(*un-SAY-vuh-ree*)
ADJECTIVE: Unpleasant or unappetizing; immoral.

He that studieth revenge

keepeth his own wounds

green, which otherwise

would heal and do well.

—JOHN MILTON

unseemly

(*un-SEEM-lee*)

VERB: Unbecoming or inappropriate; uncouth.

uxoricide

(*uk-SOR-ih-syd*)

NOUN: The act of murdering one's wife.

vanquish
(*VAN-kwish*)
VERB: To defeat an opponent; annihilate.

vengeance
(*VEN-juhns*)
NOUN: Inflicted punishment in retribution for a past wrongdoing; revenge.

vent one's spleen
(*vent wuhnz spleen*)
PHRASE: Annoyance or a bad temper.

vilify
(*VIL-ih-fie*)
VERB: To make false accusations or statements against someone in order to make him or her seem villainous; malign.

> *Part of her attempt at defense was to VILIFY her husband; by making him seem like a horrible person she thought she would be able to justify his murder and escape punishment.*

vindictive
(*vin-DIK-tiv*)
ADJECTIVE: Motivated by revenge; vengeful.

virago
(*vi-RAH-go*)
NOUN: A tempestuous, loud, or domineering woman.

virulent
(*VEER-yuh-lent*)
ADJECTIVE: A person or thing that is extremely hostile or poisonous; bitter.

vitriolic
(*vit-ree-OL-ik*)
ADJECTIVE: Characterized by hate or spite; acerbic.

vituperative
(*vie-TOO-per-uh-tiv*)
ADJECTIVE: Behavior or speech that is insulting and abusive; slanderous.

volatile
(*VOL-uh-tull*)
ADJECTIVE: Prone to sudden changes or outbursts; unpredictable.

> *The situation with their government is VOLATILE; it's unwise to travel there until we know exactly what is going to happen.*

wangle
(*WANG-gul*)
VERB: To manipulate a situation through deceit or trickery; finagle.

> *She was easily able to WANGLE her way out of being charged with theft by crafting a story interesting enough to distract the investigator.*

wary
(*WAYR-ee*)
ADJECTIVE: Suspicious or leery.

waspish
(*WAH-spish*)
ADJECTIVE: Easily irritated or bothered; spiteful.

wrathful
(*RATH-full*)
ADJECTIVE: Full of anger or spite; enraged.

wrest
(*rest*)
VERB: To take something away from someone using force.

wroth
(*roth*)
ADJECTIVE: Wrathful or spiteful.

Anger is one of the sinews

of the soul; he that wants it

hath a maimed mind.

—THOMAS FULLER

X, Y, and Z

Xanthippe

(*zan-TIP-ee*)

NOUN: A reference to Socrates' wife, a *Xanthippe* is a shrewish, ill-tempered woman.

yahoo

(*YAH-hoo*)

NOUN: A crude, coarse, or brutish person. In Swift's *Gulliver's Travels*, one of a race of brutes having the form and all vices of humans.

yell

(*yel*)

VERB: To cry out of scream with anger, fright, or pain.

yob

(*yob*)

NOUN: A thug or hooligan.

> *You may run to the store around the corner, but watch out for the YOB hanging by the door; he's likely to knock you down and take your money.*

yuck

(*yuhk*)

INTERJECTION/SLANG: An expression of strong dislike or disgust.

zap
(*zap*)
VERB: To kill; to shoot; to attack or destroy with sudden speed and force.

zounds
(*zoundz*)
INTERJECTION: Used to express anger or indignation.

DAILY BENDER

Want Some More?

Hit up our humor blog, The Daily Bender, to get your fill of all things funny—be it subversive, odd, offbeat, or just plain mean. The Bender editors are there to get you through the day and on your way to happy hour. Whether we're linking to the latest video that made us laugh or calling out (or bullshit on) whatever's happening, we've got what you need for a good laugh.

If you like our book, you'll love our blog. (And if you hated it, "man up" and tell us why.) Visit The Daily Bender for a shot of humor that'll serve you until the bartender can.

Sign up for our newsletter at
www.adamsmedia.com/blog/humor
and download our Top Ten Maxims No Man Should Live Without.